Hour of the Pearl

HOUR OF THE PEARL
RHONA McADAM

THISTLEDOWN PRESS

Canadian Cataloguing in Publication Data

McAdam, Rhona, 1957-
    Hour of the Pearl
Poems.

ISBN 0-920633-26-9 (bound).
ISBN 0-920633-27-7 (pbk).

I. Title.
PS8575.A53H6 1987 C811'.54 C87-098026-2
PR9199.3.M32H6 1987

Book design by A. M. Forrie
Silkscreens and photographs by Djavid Mostame

Typeset by Pièce de Résistance, Edmonton
Set in 11 point Caslon 540

Printed and bound in Canada by
Hignell Printing Ltd., Winnipeg

Thistledown Press Ltd.
668 East Place
Saskatoon, Saskatchewan
S7J 2Z5

Acknowledgements

Some of these poems have been published in the following periodicals: *Arc, Ariel, Atlantis, The Brentonian Newsletter, Canadian Forum, Canadian Woman Studies/les cahiers de la femme, Cross-Canada Writers' Quarterly, Dandelion, event, The New Quarterly, NeWest Review, Quarry,* and *Waves;* in the anthology *Writing Right: Poetry by Canadian Women;* and broadcast on CBC's "Alberta Anthology".

This book has been published with the assistance of the Alberta Foundation for the Literary Arts, the Canada Council, and the Saskatchewan Arts Board.

CONTENTS

I. FAMILY LINES

II. DOMESTIC HAZARD

III. THE SHAPE OF DESIRE

IV. DREAMING A PLACE

I. FAMILY LINES

Yolanda approaches thirteen with a new haircut;
the style I don't understand but the need for it
I remember, waiting for a generation
to establish itself, give itself form.

Yolanda approaches thirteen with magic,
with subterranean lights shining from her skin.
She's finding someone new inside, building herself
layer upon layer, seeking a spirit
strong and beautiful and perfect,
holding up possibilities to the light,
finding translucence where she wants clarity.
Questions are surfacing now
that no one can answer.

Yolanda approaches thirteen with hesitation,
facing the uncertain boundaries
she must cross alone. Tonight
she fills the house with music,
sings into the ear of her friend
pressed to telephone
a few houses away; struts
into the teens
with all she has.

There are lights shining behind her eyes; she wakes
into a day of wing and sun, an ocean of whitecaps and sea birds.

She balances on the last step of childhood; all summer
it goes like this. She is too young, even for these men,
who come for weekends from the mainland. Around her
couples join and separate, weekend upon weekend;
she is permitted to watch like a participant.

Afternoons, she swims with her mother.
They dive in smooth waters, float on logs
caught in currents that lead to open sea.
She learns to sail, scooping wind from waves,
spells elaborate semaphore to her mother on shore.

In the evenings, the guests light fires on the beach,
roast corn, shellfish, bury bottles in the water to chill.
She drinks with them, young expert,
paddles phosphorescence when she goes to fetch beer,
fascinated by the living stars that move
beneath the surface of the water, fall from her scooped hands.

It is a summer of learning, of being put upon
for the first time. She feels the first insistence
of would-be lovers, the first shove of resistance to her refusal;
knows so much better than they that it is not her time,
not her season; her blood sings simpler melodies
than theirs. She needs nothing from them now; they let her be.

Once her mother throws a party; they chill beer
in a washtub filled with ice, buy cheese, sausage,
make party trays. Someone lights a fire. There is music.
When their guests drift into the night, joined at the hands
or waist, the daughter cleans up and goes to bed.
It is the first party she's given. It has been the night
of her first kiss, a casual buss from a middle-aged salesman
who flies in drunk on alternate weekends.

Beginnings like these become only bridges to later years.
The image of these months she will carry with her
is her mother, drifting out to sea
in their yellow life raft. Stranded herself,
she stands on the deck of a sailboat, broken mast
trailing behind her on the water, watching
as the life raft floats through the limits of her vision
carrying her mother, who is reading as she drifts
through the summer afternoon, awaiting rescue.

I looked up to find the clouds moving
low and hard in the wind, the sky a dull metal grey.
I looked up to find the summer past
to see my face in the window, an old face
its grief hardly spent, a face that remembers
my boy's face in its shape, in the way the eyes are set,
certain expressions I catch, walking past mirrors.

My boy was so newly a man, at an age both fragile
and painfully tough. But he seemed all right.
So at night we cast back in our darkness
for clues we should have seen, lie separate
in the long shared silence of feigned sleep.
This finds us somehow together and apart, united
and sundered by grief we never dared imagine,
a secret evil that slipped into both of us
the thin blade of a word we can't say.

My boy rides his bike through my mind, his face
a wide summer smile, a child invisibly different from the rest.
I need reasons, a reason. I need to know the something
that was so wrong he had to kill it
to keep us from knowing. He never warned us,
let us find the sanctuary of distance. No,
he let us be close and ordinary, stole from us
the knowledge of which casual parting would be significant,
let us leave him here, alone with a death
that might have seized him even as we drove away.

My boy is newly gone; his sharp scent lingers
in the room he left forever only weeks ago.
In here he hatched ideas for harmless things;
it was these walls he leaned against
in misery, anger; this bed he leapt upon
in joy, dreamed upon in the first
terrible throes of love.
It could have been here the sadness reached
to hold him, muttered desperate comfort in his ear.

It will take time to heal the sounds
still suggesting themselves in the wind,
in the branches that knock against windows.
My boy is gone and winter comes early this year.
I am afraid of all the things time will reveal
as it melts away their hiding places.
The skis and Christmas stockings, the tea mug
and motorcycle; these things I can lay my hands upon
and remove, but I fear the inevitable discovery
one day of a toy, a letter, a stray sock;
one day when all the rest is accounted for, one of these
will reveal itself and in its ordinary
solitary presence strike me down.

In this picture you smile benignly for my camera.
I hear again the sound of your typewriter; its echoes
fill the pages of your letters when I unfold them,
tobacco-sweet from your pipe. When I visit I find
we've begun to share the interests of adults,
speak of books and films, of people we both know by first names.
But somehow these things only frame the distance between us.
I find myself wanting explanations for the empty centre
of our picture, the one that develops of shared blood.

I have my stubborn memories of us, know you as the man
behind the camera, a presence as implicit and enduring
as the images of me swinging on the gate of our past,
bouncing on the bridge of your legs between
chair and footstool, lying in your lap to hear stories
reverberate from your chest; elsewhere I am frozen in the square
of your camera's eye feeding animals in the zoo,
beckoning to you with unknown words caught in my throat.

Some part of me recalls you in those bright
sepia days I see in the old album, so lean and happy
posed with family and friends, all the photos
carefully placed on the stiff black pages; some part of me
returns my gaze in the old portraits of people
none of us can name, but whose faces bear the faint marks
of relatives, the similarity I've learned to sense
but cannot place precisely on features, a skill of grandmothers.

The photos of your mother line the drawers in my old room
there for me to dwell on when I visit, seeking some resemblance
but find us both missing from her face. I turn the pictures over
and the mirror of your script describes the time and place;
a precise and legible hand that predicts the evolution of my own.
In the end I sit and write you letters full of questions I know
will never be answered, while you invoke your library of albums
that hold only the recorded past.

I pick from the table your letter, arrived this morning.
With hands veined like yours I turn over the envelope,
stationery I bought you one Christmas.
I hear your voice in my head as I read, understanding
perfectly
                    when you say this
it means you've been ill
                    when you say that
it means you're depressed it means you feel
                                        alone.

As I grow older your features settle on my face;
my body dissolves into family lines. There are ancestors
shaping me now whom no one remembers, whom my mouth, my knees,
my oddly-shaped ankles recollect on their own.
These the long dead pattern me, are used as explanations
for characteristics no one living wants to claim.
They are answer and excuse for family ills; they lie
unacknowledged beneath the surface of conversations
that are only current variations
of family obsessions. We are a marked species
shouldering a weight we don't recognize.

In this family we talk to ourselves,
fill the hallways with whispers.
Ancestors bend our ears with their silence
while we mutter away the present,
fill the spaces between us with unshared context.

Our conversations with each other only nibble
the edges of what binds us. We don't mention
ties deeper than name, turn faces away
from each other, superstitious about mirrors.

But to ourselves, our hushed eloquence offers a means
to voice the unspeakable;
articulates a fervor of blood we reveal to the world
in a pulse at the throat, a vocabulary
nurtured by silence. In this way we can live
with ourselves; honesty exists for us
though swept beneath the spoken world,
turned to the mind's eye.

This house is a community of silence,
a rational order that links the distance
we keep. We balance time against pain,
cover our wounds with dust,
a comfort that demands immobility
and a pact of silence.

And when my sister was born there was no flagpole left
to hoist a flag up and forget until it blew tatters
of blue and red out to sea, and so my father bought
a television set; a shuttered box of glass sleeping
in the corner of the living room, waiting
for my father's touch to life. My brother
was afraid of it at first, ran from the room, thinking
only ghosts could be so grey, so humming,
so flickering on the walls.

My sister was the first among us to grow up thinking
that box belonged here as much as the chesterfield,
the fireplace. She had special rights of access,
learned to turn it on before she could walk,
named her dolls Big Show, Razzle Dazzle,
Ed Sullivan. When I was starting to date
she was hunched over homework and Star Trek
lying at the feet of Captain Kirk, or doing dishes
while in the next room Marshall Dillon
was lying wounded in the arms of Miss Kitty;
when she played with her friends it was
Superman leaping from trees with her bath towel
tucked in the back of her swimsuit.

My sister's life is arranged on the top
of the family tv. Her graduation and wedding photos
pose among the cards she sends on special occasions.
The cactus she gave my mother blooms periodically
from the mechanical heat; my mother plucks the wilted blooms
before they fall. My parents call this the family room.
It is where we gather after Sunday meals
our seats grouped around the tv's dead eye,
its crown of flowers and photographs
and we speak of my sister across the ocean
who lives now without electricity
and we wonder how she is getting on.

Behind all that silence, those years of locked doors
and solitude, you lived and considered. Now the silence cracks
around your smile, spreading more freely than before.
You have come, these past few years, almost close enough
to touch again.

The photograph of you I like best, of the few of them
you've allowed, is the one I took when I was twelve,
you thirteen, smiling from the roof of our house
where you stood perfectly straight, holding a plastic daisy.
You were smiling as you never would after that.
It must have been around the time I nearly shot you
with the bow and arrow, or when you speared my leg
with a dart. Those days we had begun to build our spaces:
you, tunneling mine shafts into the river bank,
building fences and lookout towers along the property line,
me planting my small lawn, burying pets
and their victims, both of us shutting our eyes
to the outside, looking to each other.

Now I watch you with the cat on your knee,
your long fingers passing over her coat,
hands that look like mine, but scarred
where the chisel slid into the skin of your finger
in grade eight, and you had stitches that were gone
before you could show me when I came home at Christmas.
Your few letters to me when I went away to school:
the intricate pictures, delineating the tiny forms of tanks
launching missiles to explode the clouded form
that was titled with my name. Young insults
that formed the core of our private language.
We speak now as adults, but the words are still few
and break the surface only by insinuation.
The letters that pass between cities carry our careful words
in paths outside family lines; we have spent years
inching toward each other, hoping the common ground will hold.

Last time I saw you we were all thirteen,
helping you escape from boarding school.
You were skinny and tough, dirty blonde,
passing back that last cigarette,
slipping under the gate, thumb already cocked,
pockets stuffed with supplies
for the twenty miles or so to Chemainus.

You took three of us there one Sunday,
sneaked cigarettes, one beer to share.
We giggled in the dark
and rainy field behind your house
wearing our new and leather textured jeans,
our black oxfords
polished for morning chapel
slurping through the mud.

It was supposed to be romantic. It was supposed to be
an easy thing, this flight into the big world
of men and women dancing on polished floors. Instead,
of course instead, it was a parade
through the staff lounge under the eye of the headmistress,
who checked skirt lengths for decency's sake;
instead of a respite from uniform
it was the substitution of white dresses
for green tunics. On the bus, seeking the dark-eyed
lustre of glamour, we became furtive cosmeticians,
glowing whitely through the night, dextrous
with mascara and rouge by flashlight.

At the boys' school we spilled from the bus,
incandescent in the light from the gym's open door,
lurching across gravel on feet more accustomed to oxfords.
We glowed against the wall bars with sweat and rouge,
mimicking steps in the shadows, awaiting discovery
and the fearful sheen of the dance floor.

Sooner or later we were led out to the bushes
where our dresses glowed indiscreetly
and we tasted gin and cigarettes
the better to glide into the rough hands of rugby players,
press lips and braces against lips and braces,
perhaps allow small indiscretions of touch,
exchange names and grades, home towns,
then tottered back to the gym where sooner or later
the last waltz, the last grope,
the bored chaperone's beckoning hand
as the last of us were cut from the milling, suited forms
who turned pink faces and hands
up to the school bus windows, waving from the shadows
as we jerked and tumbled into the night
to fib and gossip and begin the long hope for phone calls.

After a few months at the school
she became sharp, an instrument of listening,
ear tuned to the exact pitch of the seductive ring
that permeated the evening meal.

Even from the farthest corner
beyond the preliminary floor-creaks and dish-chimes;
even in a hall jammed with a hundred girls
eating and talking and filling the room floor to ceiling
with their noise, even then she could hear it
from the first ring; and following, the other sounds
caught among the rest, the quick scrape
of the mistress' chair as she rose, the brief
groan of the floor as she rounded the corner,
the abrupt end to the sound as she picked up the phone
in mid-ring; then her return, the name whispered
to the headmistress, her finger tapping the bell for silence,
the pause, as she waited for the noise to subside, then announced
someone else's name.

Once she did have a phone call
but failed to recognize her own name
and had to be called twice;
eagerly she lumbered to the small room
where her mother's voice rose to her ear
as familiar and out-of-place a sound
as her own name had been. Never for her
the envious taunts and winks bestowed on the golden ones
whose names were called almost daily, who walked languorously
to answer the distant longing of boys from other schools
who came to visit in blazers and flannels, strolling
the grounds on Sunday afternoons, looking younger
or more pimply than they had at the dance
but there nonetheless.

In these ten years we have ridden time's spiral
shedding young dreams, none of us
truly adrift or truly found until today
when we meet as adults, the years itching
under our skins as memory plants its cells
in changed faces
and we touch, gentle as lovers meeting
after all our lives have thrown between us.

We meet, the old connections discarded
and we become siblings, the offspring
of time and change, the ones
between whom grows something more than interest,
an affection drawn from shared histories.

We are no more than strangers who have passed
the need for introduction,
the preliminaries dispensed with in a time
when anything was possible, except this,
our meeting ten years away.

In our eyes we are each the best we could have hoped for,
and tonight our conversation floods the shadows
from lives that cannot be eclipsed.

You're gone. Somehow we've slipped apart;
I'm left staring your absence in the face.

In old photographs you appear so impassive
I question my memories of you
erupting into unexpected violence, small things
really, a deck of cards flung in my face,
a basketball slung at too sharp an angle.
And what you told me too, those things seem unreal
but I'm left with images of you
standing poised on a bridge's railing,
being thrown down your own stairs one night
into the rain with blood on your face,
watching your strung-out lover
take to the streets
later you took flowers
to the hospital, to the woman with your name
your heart caught up in her eyes, the one
I never met.

There's a gap between us, always there
in distance, yes, and the directions we face.
Do you remember hating yourself so much
braver than me, I could never go as far as you;
you were the real thing, moving hand in fist into the black
and back again, always, strength seeping out somehow.

I can't judge the value of accumulation any more
or know if it's enough to bridge ideologies
but ten years ago we were friends
and there was nothing we could not say.
This year for the first time on your birthday
I don't know how to reach you, or
which of us will be strong enough to gather the years
in her hands, and spread them again between us.

It seems we've been shedding
the skin of friendship for years now,
displacing the years of closeness,
driving between us husbands,
lovers, children; the different worlds
we move in, closed to each other

What we had lives on in photos.
You inhabit my albums, little changed,
but the context has been lost
and only the image remains:
figures pausing in conversation
frozen in gestures we no longer use

Friends are the hardest to leave behind
with the past; still, it happens without comment,
without crisis, a gentle severance of the spirit,
a parting that goes unnoticed until
silence wells from the void
and the heart remembers.

It's not just family voices now
chanting over the wire, whispering expectations
in her solitary ear; it's not just her mother's eye
that measures her hand when she brings a new man home.
At the reunion, family pictures were fanned
in the ringed fingers of old classmates
and she was back against the gym wall
waiting to be picked, torn between a sport she didn't play
and not wanting to be last.

She's noticed a recent mannerism that has her twisting
the bare finger at night; sometimes she wakes
to scratched skin, wonders if she was holding on
or tearing off the dreamed circle.

The mirror tells her it's nearly too late, and she finds men
harder to meet, and the ones she does, harder to stand.
But she has things to do, and solitude is a friend
who asks no questions, doesn't call late at night
with a voice like whiskey, wanting to come over,
doesn't need to talk right now
about something she said last week.

She goes her own way, unable to explain her reasons for wanting
her own way; entertains visits from old lovers
that sometimes turn maudlin. It seems everyone needs this
more than she does. She knows she will always be
out of step, the odd one at parties, the one
who knows more than most about dead bolts and tire changes,
prefers to sit with the men when talk turns to pregnancy
but no more at home with football.

II. DOMESTIC HAZARD

Last night for the first time
he came to my house alone. Last night
he turned my hope liquid
and drank it down,
shone the light I'd been asking for
clear into his soul until
I had to look away, having seen
what I would not hear
there is no comfort in truth.

Last night brandished a bottle,
smashed it against the table
and waved it in my face.
Last night has come between us
the uninvited guest lingering
in the bathroom, prying in the cabinets.
Last night tells me
his real name as he nods in the chair
darkness sunk in his eyes.

Last night he stayed till morning
and never touched me with his hands
but the pale rings of his words
cover the table's surface
and they may never come out.

It's an elaborate system, a fine balance
of reward and punishment, rewards meted out
to suit the punishment she accepts, glass
by bitter glass, his fist curling round the clear
white heat of illness; her face burns with it
when she walks into the emergency ward
telling the old stories the nurses hear
every time she comes in: the doors she walks into
with enough force to knock out teeth; treacherous
stairwells that batter ribs, snap bones;
broom handles that leave the sign of fingers across her face,
constellations of thumb-prints on her thighs.

They shake their heads as they bandage
and splice what her home pulls apart,
press their lips together as she asks
the bitter dignity of public silence,
gathers up her children and her fear,
the weight of unacknowledged bruises,
the prospect of solitude and poverty.

She sews with the fragile thread of faith and memory
her idea of who he is, goes to save him,
accepts the dark weave of anger and illness
he throws so casually upon her; even now she's sure
there are a thousand ways she loves him,
a thousand ways he ties her heart in knots,
binds her to his side till she stifles,
no longer breathing
her own air.

I'm sure you see me too; when I glance back
your eyes are sweeping from my face, or your head
is turning, suddenly
                        But we arrange things
so we never meet: use opposite washrooms,
good timing, place friends and tables between us
keep the distance intact
                        You haven't changed
still the same face, the familiar way you have
of sliding into drink: it swallows you,
the real you sinks from sight, leaving this other
the hard, cold, loud one in your place, the one
who knocks glasses from the table,
shoves the people who protest
aside
        You used to cover your ears but now
you seem better at keeping the world away

Each time I see you with someone else,
all of them strangers, the kind
who don't need to get close to use you, the kind
we used to fight about
                        You used the word love
without thinking, sang it so convincingly
people thought you really knew what it was
But you and I knew, we felt the lick of danger
heard the fuse hissing
                        Truth was too dangerous
for both of us; we handled it badly; I let you
push me away, you let me be weak when you needed me
most. We walked away from each other, arms folded
lips set. It seemed safer that way.

What excuses are left us
for the days we first knew you
for what filled our eyes as we watched you
drain your glass, empty into yourself
the pain you fended off with drawn curtains,
unplugged phone, stagnant despair in the afternoon.

Which of us didn't turn away when we began to see
that no, you weren't waving, you were drowning
and all the bravado, the morning after stories
were just so much more terror
swept aside, a fear you closed your eyes to
hoping for invisibility, fear starting
in our own lives at the people we were becoming.

We are all guilty in this, for waving back
at you, affirming the lies
we were all together living; guilty
for our protestations,
no it wasn't that bad, no
we won't talk about it.
I walk with the others who want better for you
each of us holding our toy horses, our armour
of tinfoil and cardboard looking shabby already.

We are your family, each of us your mother and father
you the child we've carried home in turn
your face peaceful at last, dreaming the dream of oblivion;
each of us the niece or nephew
shrinking from the boozy affection of the uncle;
each of us the sibling whose love lies near the surface,
inexhaustible despite all, seeing in your face
the frightened image of our own
knowing it's always that close.

Often I catch myself in comforting phrases
needing the familiar when my words encroach
on your terrible strangeness.
There's no good reason for this,
I hear myself say, wondering at your heroes,
gifted inebriates, all of them.
You've built yourself a pantheon of genius
a backdrop of eccentricity into which
you hope to melt, seen and unseen
the world to marvel at your talent
magnified and gilded through the glass
you hold before your face.

Through all this I catch glimpses of you
round the edges of your disguise. No good reason
I hear myself mutter, reaching out my hand
to your image, which is always farther away than it seems.
You've been playing tricks with the light
dancing off in the shadows
leaving the brittle mirror-image in your place
untouchable, inconsistent. We circle you
join hands, see with bright eyes
the shadows around you, wanting only
to trap you into substance.

I was trying to help you, give you time
to pull out of whatever it was (left it
nebulous, a cloud that rose
between us on its own)
                              The excuses
I made for you, the way I twisted memory
to suit your perception
carried deception forward until I knew
your illness was mine
                              I never meant
to condone what you were living, but now
I ask how else you could have seen it
had you been looking, while the cloud
got ready to burst
                              Even today
I can't think what the crisis was
there were so many instants, so much
shame and fear condensing
                                        in your glass
clouds swirled in the ice, genesis
of something that held you
away from me
                              your bottles growing magic
releasing something that stank
wickedly in the pouf! of release

You hold us with your promises; we wait for success
or failure, afraid to ask, afraid to test you;
you have us in thrall, a family
breathing the thin air of your dependence
                                We step carefully
in your world, muscles relaxing in spasms as time passes
and all seems well, the horizon clear; against the past
and our better judgement we begin to hope,
close our eyes to signs that hint at something
clouding the horizon, a thunderstorm massed against the heat
of our collective need
                        You break, the storm
upon us again. You are its eye, malevolent
in failure, guilt gusting to anger as you whirl
through the house, catch at our legs
suck at the ruins
                        This time we crouch
away from you; this time we have taken precautions
heeded storm warnings. We shield ourselves from you
huddled and desperate for warmth
                        The storms you bring
are not to be weathered; we must leave you to rage
we may see you burst into brilliance
and a darkness that marks briefly
your passage

They all know what's best for me, but they can't stop
the earth from dropping away beneath my feet
or my eyes, drawn to his face,
to the door he might enter.
They don't see me run to him in secret
when he comes back, right to his arms
when I've sworn I'll stay away, don't see me
stalking him, need clenched in my pockets,
my arms become naked wings and me
the flimsy insect beating against glass
his face gazing from the frame or hidden
behind windows. He's swallowed me,
sucked my reason dry but my fists still echo
against the glass and he is apart from me,
one foot at least in another world.

He comes to me in anger, need
or drink, and with his fists grounds me, my hope
that this time it's as he says, different;
but all he does is drive me further down,
the pain so great now I can't feel
anything but the lack of him,
don't miss the everything that having him
has taken away. This love will kill me.
I feel it at night when I watch him walk
away, my hands against the window
framing his shape as it disappears
and I stand with my palms against ice
and the thin pane that holds me here.

III. THE SHAPE OF DESIRE

This evening has grown wings that brush
the tips of feathers against my heart,
spreading the outline of your face,
blurring the strokes with which you've drawn yourself
so suddenly into my life. Another heartbeat
to remember now, a star pulsing behind my eyes
when I stare into darkness, listening for your voice
as the trees groan outside the window and release
the gold birds of autumn to fly
blind as night against the glass.

The leaves will lie where they fall tonight.
I am fixed on other things, no longer want
to measure this distance across water,
through the shining coils of your city,
or mark the things that lie between us
in what has gone unsaid and unplanned
except in the tentative glance you offered,
the shy weight of arms circling like old friends.
Only my heart might hear these new songs
pitched high above one more night of questions
while I sing you to life by asking them.

Falling in love with you
I am the blind musician
placing my hands on the stove
to play the final circles of pain
before the larger music of your body
is all I feel.

i.

Last night I dreamed
your cheek upon my pillow
reached my hand to touch
the dark planes of your skin
saw your eyelash sweep
its brief arc across your face
before I woke

ii.

We watch each other, we both know it, but dance
delicate and separate away from each other's sight
each holding the other in our minds
in a grip so naked the blood rushes in our ears
and we behave as if deaf, carelessly vague
to conversations that weave themselves
between us, to which we nod assent, pausing
as if to consider, but looking down only
to look over. Once I catch your eyes
the room so reflected in your gaze
I can't meet your look and turn
my longing deflected.

I'm afraid of what lights the air
between us, afraid others will see
the charge that arcs
when your hand brushes mine, reaching
for cream or sugar, something innocuous
to ground this feeling.

The music takes me in its arms
and at last I can move
closing my eyes to feel your lips brush
my lids; blindness holds such promise
I could burn here forever and none would see.

in the afternoon, through cool air
green and gold tangle in branches
moving against sky, blue
altitude of light framing the room

slung in the branches, saxophone
slides on green trees, filling the window
leaves wave golden hands into reflections
fling themselves into air

moving against blue
he loses himself in the exploding
jungle of her body

breezes scatter against the screen
in the bed beneath the window
their bodies applaud each other
birds sing their way to the tops of trees
music floats from the room to the sky

Tonight my love grows wings
and flutters around your door
with the furious energy of obsession;
tonight I find you walking outside
and tangle myself in your hair, rest on your neck
a light finger's caress, follow you
so tall, slim, fair as any candle
slip in your door in the wake
of your passage.

Tonight the white wings of my love
whisper through your sleep till you rise
to see what the noise is, cup me
helpless in your hands, step outside
fling me skyward, to where the stars
outline my desire and I wheel, dizzy
with space and cold air, descend again
to wheel, rapturous around your light
beat my wings against the hard door of refusal.

Tonight my wings are the colour of sand
and I lie in camouflage against your door
my body pressed to the pane between us.
In the morning you look outside
no memory of my presence;
in the morning you gaze unknowing
through the frosted shape of desire.

Tonight I am of the beasts of the backyard
my face is one of the multitude gazing upwards
at your window, I am one of the rumbling
furred assembly living to twine about your legs
when you step out and among us in the morning

Tonight I am the wild love running
and rampaging through your flower garden
chasing for the pure speed of it
the small competitors for your favour
returning happy, panting to wait for you

Tonight I scratch at your door
behind which you lie sleeping
somewhere in the dark civilized recesses
wherein I would burst in a frenzy of passion
to envelop you in my affection
the nuzzling, love-thrumming love
of beast for beast

You are as winter to me; the warm spot in the bed
left by the cat's sleeping, the taste of tea
on a cold afternoon, a palm curled on my cheek
against snow, against wind.
Yours is the arm I join with mine
while the season calls down its signs around us.

Listen: my boots speak your name's syllables
in snow so cold the flakes rasp underfoot
or there, I hear you overhead
in the trolley lines' distant static.
You are everywhere in these margins of ice.
When I breathe in the needled air
your scent tickles the last moment, elusive
and my breath shapes you bit
by clouded bit in ice crystals
and a sun of brushed silver.

You are my camera / my body turns to you
in the light / you hold shadows and scatter
petals of darkness on my skin / I turn to you
am swallowed in the widening lens
of your presence / you still me with a soft sound
this moment stops / you reach out and hold me
chiaroscuro in your eye / I am reduced to black and white
you pattern me / in shades of grey
shape my soul in variations of light

You are my camera / in you is all I could want to see
you take my face in your hands / and we slide into view
our lives a tunnel / step and repeat the vision
lives tripping over each other / moments separated
by time and space and angle / regular lives expanding

You are my camera / hold my secret lives inside
where only time can loose them / in your hands
through the brief moments of your fingers / I slip
rich and dark as you make me / I smile back
into your face / meet your eyes
draw a sepia gaze / we slip
into the deep grain of this moment

you are so thin   so thin I dip
my fingers in the grooves between your ribs
pad the angles of your hips
with my own   your skin
so loose it almost peels away
so pale   colour of bone

your face is a frame   curved
to hold your eyes   a face
pulled into odd corners   shadowed hollows
meant for candlelight   or stars
I touch the evening's beach of bone and skin
completely   as the sand might

From time to time I watch you closely, with new eyes,
appreciating how much of you I haven't seen

and I'm no longer sure whether it's what I know of you
that attracts me, or what I might find.

When we met, I thought knowledge had limits, that in love
we were finite beasts who shared known boundaries

but watching you touch objects for which I have no desire
I see a measure of longing in your eyes

that forces me to say, I don't know you yet. That forces me
to say, there are places in you I may not wish to know.

In love we are beasts of infinity, crude in our longing
for things that may carry us apart. It's more than biology

or romance, more than drawing thorns from feet
with gentled fangs, more than all we have been told;

it's finding a reason to come together
without killing the wildness we each carry

like a gift we haven't decided to share
and hold inside ourselves with only the edges showing.

Our boats part in the strait
reaching arms of light
across black water, until distance
and the humped back of the island intervene.
Ahead of me other lights
cast white ropes to my feet
pulling me home.

I ride this night of diesel and salt
outside, with the wind on my face,
my thoughts on you.
We have been cautious this trip,
moving among friends and family
promising nothing. We will meet again
a thousand miles from now,
move back into cherished routines,
creeping closer on the shared threads
of this journey, dancing the future
on the decks of different ships.

Her face has been framed by the kitchen window
for as long as she can remember. She watches
him pull off his shirt, swing the axe
in palms swollen with callous. All of him out there
is focussed on the tree stump he is wresting from the earth.
He doesn't look up, not once, just flows with the tool,
base of an arc of metal and bone. She nips the ends
of vegetables, no longer afraid of the nicks and scrapes
that bloom from time to time on palm and finger;
her hands are a fine network of scars and burns,
emblems of her position here, poised behind the window.

At first she'd tried to participate, lent her clumsy strength
to the tasks he started. But her hands blistered,
bled into the thin gloves she wore, and she was awkward
with the heavy tools he seemed to wield by instinct.
There was no grace in her movements, no sure placement
of steel and wood; he grew impatient, pushed her back,
gently pushed her back to the kitchen window
than hangs between them like law.

Now and then she brings him coffee, food.
He takes it but his mind tangles on the roots
still hidden beneath the earth, holding the base of a tree
that first shed leaves the season she was born.
The sheared trunk's pale surface is marked
with a sudden ring of red, too human a colour
for an ordinary afternoon like this.

Her chest tightens with every bite of the axe
and when the stump at last gives to the blade,
shaking with each blow, she turns away
not hearing the falling away of earth
as the last roots snap and release,
and she wonders if he will look up then
and see the window empty.

IV. DREAMING A PLACE

I was content here till you ignited me with your talk
of lands I've never seen, spoke of them
as of disease for which you're grateful,
with which you languish happily
returning again and again to the countries
that feed the fever and inflame it
the moment you turn your back.

You've infected me with your talk
of the mountains, the gods parting the clouds
the people who dance and sing till morning.
I've begun to burn, toss in my sleep
crave foods I've never tasted
hum tunes with foreign beats
wake to the sounds of words
my lips form without understanding.

In my native cold
I shiver unaccountably nothing will warm
my blood it flows thick and slow
this disease spreading through my veins
your talk reverberating in my head
                                    my bones
grow into new shapes I am transformed
transfixed fit for nothing in my world
words for motion travel fill me up
                                    my feet
feel the floor like strangers long to kick off
the bindings that hold them here want to MOVE
with the beat of an equatorial dance want to
move among strangers of other lands want to feel
the fire of their sun have the fever inside
around me chasing away the bland chill of this life

i.

All around me abandoned journeys
whisper their troublesome words into the ears
of friends and lovers,
         keep at them for years, say
how could you leave me like this, you haven't lived
till you've seen me through. The abandoned journeys
make deals which strike me as unethical:
         Come back to me
the journeys say, baring a thigh, come back
and I will give you peace; come back, without me
you are nothing.
         And they listen to that
when at home I can offer them
pâté and conversation. They pack their bags
and board planes destined for airports
whose names sprawl across their tickets
in the hieroglyph of fulfillment
and I'm certain as they leave,
         as the plane lifts off
and I wave into nothing, they will be back
eyes ringed like addicts;
I will see their faces and know it's not the end
they are footloose, they are wild, wild creatures,
they will not be tied to expectation.

ii.

The abandoned journeys
wave cheekily at me from travel posters. They thumb
well-tanned noses and cling daintily
to the bronzed arms of my beloved
who faces away from the camera
not wanting to be caught.
                              I am filled with fear
for the ones I love, rage against travel ads
dream of starting a movement whose purpose
is as pure as gospel. Soon I will stop these men
in their tracks, appeal to their need
for higher purpose. I will best the abandoned journeys
teach them respect for the family unit.

Soon too I will still the undulating
call of the islands my last lover
slipped in my vein with his warm brown fingers
one night last winter when I shivered in
from a long day at the office, a long drive
in the frozen city. This is my home, I have known
all along that winter does not last forever
I am strong, I can live for summer, I know the way

        aloha

You must travel light these days,
jettison the heart's blind baggage
to the careless shoulders of roads
who shrug the bounce and rattle of names
that need forgetting, lips that came too close.

You've only room for one on this trip
that never ends; you pause for rest
alone, never wanted hands circling your wrists
when you'd only asked the way,
never expected the words that were whispered
when you stopped to get directions.

Your friends are strangers, your lovers faceless
in the dark nights of other countries.
There is nothing lost in giving yourself away
in small pieces. It all comes back together
in the mirror you make of all the shards
strangers deflect; how can they be wrong
about you when they've not come close enough
to lose perspective.

Tonight rain falls lightly, freezing on pavement.
She watches the road, leaning into the wheel
as shadows fall over themselves
on the empty seat beside her. She accelerates
leaving the parting behind her, a distance she measures
on the light poles sliding past with their shadows.

Had it been daylight she would be feeling
the shadow of the plane on her back,
a large silence crossing her path.
But tonight there is rain and dark
and he is removed from her in the warm
bright cabin, tended by smiling women
who will not confuse him with intimacy,
just see to his comfort, then withdraw
into the humming night above the clouds.

His destination he has packed and taken with him
leaving her the crumpled paper and dirty plates,
the damp towel of his passage. She cannot imagine
where he has gone, his trip planned for so long
and now so suddenly upon her. She's not sure
what to do as she swings the door open
into darkness, nameless shapes of his absence.

Now he's gone
to do what his life requires of him, she's left
nursing her nobility, her unwillingness to stand
between him and what he thinks he needs to do.
She doesn't like the emptiness men's adventures leave
in the arms of women, or to understand
a plane ticket is worth more than she is.
Small comfort to call him a hero if he stayed:
that's not his vocabulary. And who needs
to be blamed later when he can't find
peace within himself, just an empty hole
he thinks adventure would have filled.

When he told her he
had to go he used words like fulfillment,
life-dream, essential. He spoke of needs, incompleteness,
not wanting to regret. He treated her to glimpses of worlds
he intended to conquer, unfolded bright handfuls of colour.
Brochures he must have been collecting for months
spilled across the table, not quite enough
to bridge the space between them.

She imagines him today hang gliding
the Himalayas, or crossing anonymously
the unfamiliar borders of a country
she's unable to imagine, whose food and language
are beyond her senses. He moves among the people,
a tall, pale god, his mind on everything but her.
She'll be the little piece of romance he's stowed away
behind his eyes to make him look worldly, bereft;
the hint of forlorn sadness he'll use to lure
other women to his side. He'll offer a damaged love,
crippled by hard life choices; never ask
what glint of sadness their eyes conceal,
wives of the argonauts, widows of Indiana Jones.

It must have arrived this morning, nestled smugly all day
in her mailbox with bills and flyers, creased and warped
from the weeks of snow and distance it crossed to reach her.
She would have missed it as she stood over the garbage can
dealing out the junk mail, but for the stamps, waving
bright hands from the paper's blue sky.

She takes the blade in her hands, makes the ritual slit,
the ritual tear that disjoints the ends of two sentences.
She unfolds his words, wanting and not wanting something more
than glib descriptions of monuments, carefully poignant accounts
of the people whose lives he's pilfered for detail.
She reads without finding one word about the two of them,
finds no clue to his heart's whereabouts. She places the letter
with the others, still wondering what they mean,
what he means her to do with them.

She fingers the winter clothes he left with her,
tries to recall how the two of them must have looked
walking together in snow, turning to each other
faces bleak with the season's pallor.
Now she sees her face growing webbed with time and climate,
while in her mind, his face grows tan, his eyes shine
the colour of aerogrammes, his skin grows smooth
as polished cotton, forgives the years
winter fabric scratched into him.

Her window frames empty streets
slick with cold, littered with the frozen skeletons
of leaves that hunch in gutters like abandoned postcards.
The familiar shape of winter scuttles beneath the window,
whispers his name over and over until it becomes
the foreign language she must unlearn.

His departure has lengthened into absence.
She turns his picture face down on her desk,
stops counting the growing gap between postcards,
no longer worries their exiguous details for meaning.

She stretches herself beyond his implied presence
at her side, turns over their years together
gingerly, expecting the rank underbelly of something dreadful
but finds instead something small and old and frightened
something with the dull gleam of neglect
disappearing in the light.

Should he return there are words they will have to exchange
and she hopes there will be no need
for elaborate posturing. Surely somewhere
in the long nights of his travels he has arrived
at an honest ending he can bring back to her
something they can share.

So many planes, all these hallways, so long
they taper into distance, walled by windows.
I keep seeing your figure at the point
where these lines meet, at the end
of someone else's journey there you are
a traveller's mirage, a focal point
I long to find, my journey over and you to hold.

Between the heads of strangers I look for you in crowds
graceful as an athlete, always in balance,
expect your gaze to rise from another's brow.
I'm always wanting a fixed point to circle,
and I've chosen quicksilver, you the heavy waters
I'll lose myself in whenever I find you.
For now though I'm free as air, I'm tied to you in thought
your hands still pattern my skin, yours is the face
forming in the clouds beyond the jet's wingtips, another
pale horizon this life carries me past. And so I unfold
the small table from where it nests in the seat before me,
take up this pen and write you back into sight,
call you from your day into my hungry corners
on another trip out of town; slowly your head
becomes visible in someone's seat a few rows away,
your voice forms my name from the sound the engines make
and by the time the plane lands I can see you again
in the crowd clustered at the landing gate.

So often I'm caught between poles of wanting you
and wanting this life, of needing you near me and never looking
beyond the ticket's path, following only what leads
to another town, another airport, another long distance
call to you, wondering where I am, where you are
pulling me home with your voice while I pull papers
from my case and know there's one more flight I must take
through skies that finally spell your name to me
in the single points of light spilling in my wake.

After it's over she rests
hands flat on the desk
sees the shape of them
spread-eagled on the dark veneer,
a pair of children dreaming
a place in the new neighbourhood.

This man was the first
of many people whose lives
she will wrench in new directions;
her heart still sounds its message
—there are things I don't know
about this. From her place
in the organization she watched
the man's lips move from aquiescence
to anger, swam backwards in herself
seeking eyes that see nothing, the place
where the mind finds absolute simplicity
clings to it like a limpet
protected from reason.

I look at the sky and wonder how long
before the dark clouds come, bend my head again
to the earth and the knots of weeds
wrestling against my pull
as I make my will known in the garden.

There's no comparing this garden with those of my neighbours
whose orderly rows of green and soft brown earth
stand testament to a heritage of bent backs and stained palms;
ancestral gardens, terraced hillsides spreading
green and black beneath hot suns, distant mountains,
tended with the love born of hunger and ancestry,
skill passed from calloused hand to pink fist.
Now the old women tie up their hair in babushkas,
mutter their tasks in sibilants and gutturals,
cast seeds for vegetables they will preserve in the old ways
as safeguards against hunger and solitude,
jars they will fill with the colours of love
and summer, then hand to their children on visits,
or wrap in new pairs of pants or underwear
and mail across the country to the young ones
who study a new way of life.

They tend their gardens and cast looks over fences
at the likes of me, tending mine haphazardly
with my spray-can insecticide, my cotton gloves
and shiny garden tools, digging ineptly among the weeds
and the sprawling disorder of my vegetables.
The radio says there will be frost: I shrug, but my neighbours
sigh and pull out blankets and burlap, spend the afternoon
wrapping their gardens against the cold.
They stand in their gardens with umbrellas
against the hail, set out dishes of beer for the slugs,
keep cats for the birds. Always disaster
is a step ahead, its greedy hand poised
to pull away what they build.

The last days of the season she lives in a world
of steam and spice, bends her back
to the cadence of knife and board,
chopping the coloured flesh of the garden,
working long into night.
The children prop chins on the counter,
chatter in thin hungry voices that fade
as he comes in and gathers them in his arms,
takes them she knows not where
to eat she dares not imagine what
but she smiles as they pass from sight
and turns back to the stained pages before her,
sways in the rhythm of her work.
Deep into night she strains and chops
and ladles, working an alchemy of glass
that when she falls into bed beside him
he turns to her pungent body, breathes
ginger and cloves, vinegar and honey
on her skin, berries on her lips
and apples beneath her nails;
that when the children rise from their beds
and glide into the kitchen, fisting eyes into sight,
they gather round to gape at the gold, the scarlet,
the summer-grass green all gleaming
in brass-crowned rows on the counter
with lids that snap in their dreams all night.

So it is that deep into winter they taste
the sweet, edgy fruits of this night,
and she lifts one by one from the shelves
jars that shine with summer, that pattern
behind her eyes the shape of a garden she will plant
and tend and harvest, and she feels only slight regret
as the jars are emptied, to rest then in dust and darkness,
to wait for the turning of earth
and her strong hands to turn them to use.

Her feet are marching on needles
caught in the vice of seasonal flair
they are bound in leather and suede
they are pressed into sharp points that spear nothing
they are tipped upwards and propped on slender columns
that impale the meshed covers of street vents
or spike the surface of paths, not wanting to move.

Naked, her feet choose new shapes for themselves
they grow red, the bones knot at the joints,
the arches sigh and sink earthward.
On certain toes the skin thickens
into graceless lumps the professionals treat
with scalpels and acid.

Her feet leave their shapes in her shoes
press their outlines in leather
scuff their gait in her soles.
Over and over they leave their traces;
time and again she lifts them into fresh shoes
factory clean, the shape of no human appendage
and they must wear their message once more
against pavement, weather and gravity;
against reason and gender and balance.

It's deep night. Out the window, distant lights
my city-trained eye sees first as street lights
then recognizes as stars. Out here you have to forget
learned artifice, begin to relax the vigilance
your body stores against the city, against the night.
Out here it's wood smoke and tree sap,
the cold is sharp and clean, and the nights
go by without sound, a deep breath you find
yourself taking between pitch black and pre-dawn.

The city's so far behind me now I forget on what
square of its grid my home sits waiting,
full of my city clothes, my city cats
pacing the perimeter of rooms
raking claws that seek the rough
instinctive memory of bark
across my carpets. I shed the skin of that life
for the temporary sweetness of air
and uncluttered sky of this.
When I return in the morning
beneath the smooth cloth of my city self
this other will again go into waiting
to shed the accessories, and by the moon and starlight
to walk with long free strides
the earth paths that separate the trees.

At the fountain, children roll up pant legs
and advance into the cage of water, so brave
in the brilliant day, jewels cascading
over their heads to fall in the cool at their feet

People walk, truncated in reflection
from the still water on the reflecting pool.
We search the perimeter with our eyes,
pacing the borders of the water field
and find no coins, no one. Tomorrow
we will see children with masks and snorkels
cruising the area like pink sharks

It's a curious place: nothing wild grows here,
no fish, no weeds. There are paths
and stepping stones, platforms around
artificial pools and waterfalls; even the flowers
grow in regular patterns of colour and scent.
People group themselves sparsely,
just figures in an architect's drawing.
A couple reclines in bathing suits
by the shallow pool at one end,
surreal in the makeshift wilderness.

i.

Tonight I walk the High Level Bridge
for the first time in months
safe from the winter winds that coursed
along the frozen path of river and through
the bridge's metal bones. After the ready melt
of roads and lawns I am surprised that breakup
has yet to come, the river a dark thin tongue
down the white skin of ice.

ii.

A haze clouds the street lights; amber flashes
beyond the horizon. A figure advances, masked
and veiled in dust, pushing a machine that combs
winter gravel from grass. The figure advances dimly
down the middle of the road, wind sweeping dust
toward the river, the traffic island smoking in dusk.

iii.

Spring, the damp-dog smell of it scattering
in the air, streets littered with chunks of snow,
shards of ice. Drains rebel and on the corners
lakes grow where ice has choked the water's passage.

It's a time of indeterminate footwear and coats;
nothing is adequate for the weather's caprices,
but no one seems to mind. Released from wind chills
and black ice, from ice fog and ice crystals
people emerge from fur and downfill
to regain human forms; feet freed from moonboots
they walk in shoes again.
Convertables appear, braying music
as they pass over the drying pavement
driving toward summer.

It doesn't matter when it comes,
it's always early, always catches us
cursing, off-guard, one foot in our summer shoes
when we look outside to white cold.

Down the street, someone's laundry hangs on the line
become white and furred.
The young woman on night shift at the cafe
picks her way home down a street that was beige
with fall last night; her face says she doesn't believe this,
says she'll give the day time, get some rest,
let the world come to order. Children, late for school,
form the first snowball of the year, exult
in its damp roundness, in the humped shape it leaves
on fences and coats, whoop their voices
across muffled streets, show up bright as energy
against encroaching winter. The buses are late,
are required to be late each year on this day,
fishtailing through traffic, through lines of cars
peopled by suddenly timid men and women
relearning the cautions of ice, trying to remember
what they've plugged in at home
with the car's extension cord, trying to think
of this as fall. And the animals, oh the dogs
snorting in it, dashing off with noses rimed in cold,
the cats picking their feet up, and seeing
all the hiding spots are gone, they slink in the alleys
sharp and long as shadows against the day.

Each year it makes us wonder
and search horizons of snow for some green clue
that the world is alive, that something moves beyond
these banks of ice. The air settles
cold as razors on our skin, the wind finds cracks
in doors, breathes frost through windows
grown thick and hoared, obscuring signs
of life. Winter is absolute,
winter stops us dead, cars stall in roadways,
abandoned where they sit, wheels freezing
square on the road's surface.
The cold is unimaginable, binds eyelashes together,
burns cheeks and fingertips, forces
sudden springs of body fluids to the surface.
In this we wrap ourselves invisible,
lean into the wind's knives and blunder on
blind over snow packed so hard
gravel scatters in gutters
and the ice lays its flat fingers
down the length of the city.

They make you ask yourself
was this someone I know? Does this
disembodied voice belong
to a familiar face, someone I pass
blindly on the street, is this someone
whose elbow I've brushed in the elevator,
someone whose face I've glimpsed
beyond my window, curtained in darkness?

We learn to cut him off after the first words,
finger on the phone's button, precise
the click to silence. Calm, automatic,
hating that this must become routine,
that the daytime world disarms these calls
as if the commonplace lacks impact.
What of the fear they force of darkness
an unrecognizable voice sounding our names
over and over in the after-silence
our names caught in his mouth
how has he found our names

Our anger spreads over the city
a scattered rage that thins by morning
into vague mistrust. Every smiling face
mocks our interrupted sleep, each greeting
assumes the tones of deception
each accidental touch is a hand that reaches
as far as the wire can go, is the obscene contact
of a stranger's mind

She's been staring down sleep with her worry,
tossing it back sticky with fear, holding it at arm's length
while her mind turns, while she wonders
what is happening to her, tries to decide
if this is sudden or if gradually
she's come to this
                              point in her life
where gaps invade conversation
leave her groping stubbornly
for that word, an easy word, starts with
-----yes, she has it
but by now talk has drifted on without her

She's cold with this thing at night
it's something she cannot seek comfort for
She knows the words people use
when things start
                              slipping away
Uses them herself, lips moving in the dark

The doctor hands her a prescription for sleep
Resisting, she begins the groggy half-life
of the insomniac, taking the pills only
when the fatigue becomes unbearable
The drug carries its own fog

Walking to her car one afternoon she trips
on cement
                    falls
into pain, arm cushioning her weight
                                        snapping

The surgeon describes the break, names the bones
She listens, cradling pain
in the shattered elbow, fragments locked together
bound in the stiff white plaster

She no longer resists the pills
falls into the well of dreamless dark
waiting for the healing
all the weight of time upon her

It's as if she's spent her whole life
moving forward only to discover
like the illusory dance the children do, moonwalk,
she's moonwalked backwards into time
lost all the ground she gained

Fatigue catches at my sight, flecks vision
with the jumpy minutiae of strung nerves.

The neural pathways contort
as I lie in absolute

wakefulness, finding blood's stars
jerking in a ceiling I watch with closed eyes.

Sunday night, as usual, and the week sprawls
untidily, inexorably full before me

and my mind fragments, the bits scurry off
to parcel out my time, appointments

jumbling together, plans twisting backwards,
meetings running on through lunches, movies missed,

letters lost in the mail, cheques bouncing,
staff playing hooky, poems not coming together.

The rabble of thoughts gathers in my head
and clamours for attention, scratches my eyes

with red fingernails, carving "things to remember"
across my retina.

All day the cranes have been moving
slow, massive wands against the sky

Coffee break, the crane operator
crawls out of the glass egg
and along the arm, walking stooped
in the yellow network of steel

The workers sit, legs apart
dangling steel booted feet
10 storeys up;
brave enough to whistle belch and catcall
from the safety of numbers
and up there

Women in the street walk on
praying for earthquakes
and sudden winds

All night we drove the prairie
not seeing, in dark, the level fields parting
to give way to the road.
                     We should have grown close,
but were each intent on watching the road,
on thinking ahead to the men and obligations
for which we shared this flight home
in the middle of the night.
                     We never let conversation
bite into reality, kept things moving with effort
and the need to stay awake, the road fanning below
the headlights, pale and steady.
                     What we didn't know
was that sound the wheels made, the sound of something
wrong, moving with us, rolling south to north
on this highway, the sound of a wheel ready to fall,
the sound of a wheel rim carving lug nuts
into shiny hourglasses of steel
while in ignorance we prayed our routine
prayers of travel, trying to hold disaster
to the confines of the city, the place where something
can always be done.
                     Because disaster was only
promised, because we travelled that night blind
to its possibility, we engaged in no real reflection,
shared nothing but mild concern and a letter I wrote you later
to tell you what might have been.
                     All it left us
was a sense of shared possibility too unpleasant for mention,
hiding behind today's polite smiles of reacquaintance.
We turn out to be more civilized than we'd care to admit
as conversation flounders and we nod, turn back to our friends.

Night and fear clasp hands
and present themselves to my attention,
pause on the kitchen steps
to kick a piece of gravel
wispily aside.
Continuing
they shuffle faintly
through discarded newspapers
ting
on the water pipes
tap a brutal, grimy thumbnail
delicately on the sink's bare surface.
Outside my doorway they rest
breathing in
and out, shifting
from foot to foot so gently
the floor hardly creaks.
When I close my eyes they lean in
the doorway and I feel their cool breath
teasing a stray hair on my neck.
Hands still joined they soft foot it
into the living room, to sit
slowly on the old chairs, trail fingers
across the mantel, swing the hanging plant.
Just before it chimes they tap the clock
to see if it's working, then look out the window
and tease the neighbour's dog who whines
and snuffles in reply.

Enough, this ONCE I leap
bravely from bed, flashlight and reflex
at the ready, dash from room to room
flicking on lights, radio, television,
drive fear and night from the house
to crouch snickering among the bushes
below my window.

My cat is restless at night
hides in the closet
batting belts until
the hangers rattle,
crouching before me sly-eyed
darting away when I move
she feigns my assault

flings herself on the bed
worrying my blanketed foot
then casually reveals her belly
the patch of ungrown fur
showing pinkly naked
even now, a month later.
The scar is gone, no trace
of my betrayal remains
but the hairless rectangle
and the look she gives me
taking my hand in her teeth.

You reach a certain age and suddenly
everyone around you is covered with bruises;
there's hardly room for another blow.
You miss being young and vulnerable
being able to walk into anything
with your heart wide open. Still, all this damage
offers a certain protection, time toughens
around old scars, the wounds cannot be made
in exactly the same place. You learn caution,
learn to wield pain more cleverly
against others, there is a balance to be sought.

At a certain age you find yourself
looking into mirrors, into the faces
smiling back at you; you find
you're all speaking the same polite words:
what the years have taught you collapses
into what can be said. Age assumes much,
disallows so many questions,
lets you peel away pretense and reveal
the mask beneath.